FINANCIAL LONGEVITY

INCREASE YOUR WEALTH SPAN, SPEND MONEY GUILT-FREE, AND GAIN THE CONFIDENCE TO ENJOY YOUR BIGGER FUTURE

FINANCIAL LONGEVITY

INCREASE YOUR WEALTH SPAN, SPEND MONEY GUILT-FREE, AND GAIN THE CONFIDENCE TO ENJOY YOUR BIGGER FUTURE

MICHAEL MERLIN

MACMILLAN

First published in the United States in 2024 by Igniting Souls

First published in India 2026 by Macmillan
an imprint of Pan Macmillan Publishing India Private Limited
707 Kailash Building
26 K. G. Marg, New Delhi 110001
www.panmacmillan.co.in

Pan Macmillan, The Smithson, 6 Briset Street, Farringdon, London EC1M 5NR
Associated companies throughout the world
www.panmacmillan.com

ISBN 978-93-6113-389-3

1 3 5 7 9 8 6 4 2

Printed and bound in India by Thomson Press India Private Limited

DEDICATION

To my family for always inspiring
and encouraging me to follow my instincts.
To my mentors who were willing to share their wisdom
and taught me how to approach a problem or challenge.
To all those who pick up this book,
thank you for giving my words a chance,
and for continuing the worthwhile quest
for high quality financial education.

Table of Contents

Part Three: Future

Foreword

The idea of longevity—the desire to live a long, healthy, and fulfilling life—dates back to even the most ancient civilizations. While the quest for longevity has been a constant and pronounced pursuit of humankind, for many of the world's most successful entrepreneurs and innovators who remain focused on sustaining excellence, the importance of multi-generational, holistic financial planning—or "financial longevity"—often remains overlooked. That is where Michael Merlin begins his engaging book.

In *Financial Longevity*, Michael provides readers with a path for building and preserving wealth that reflects today's world, in addition to sharing valuable insight on several important habits to cultivate: the value of creating—and adhering to—a unique financial plan with a deeply experienced advisor, the importance of early and continuous financial education, and the enduring benefits of considering and involving the next generation when it comes to building a lasting legacy. As President & Chief Executive Officer of Rockefeller Capital Management, a financial advisory firm that serves some of the world's most successful individuals and families, these concepts resonate deeply with our clients.

The Rockefeller name is synonymous with multigenerational success, legacy, and the power of financial longevity. Michael understands that longevity, which along with the values that shape one's financial and life experiences, has universal meaning. Through these chapters, he provides a seasoned perspective on what it means to actively create a financial legacy that so many strive to achieve.

Greg Fleming
President & Chief Executive Officer,
Rockefeller Capital Management

PART ONE
Foundation

CHAPTER ONE

The Diagnosis

The Persians ruled the world when stories of a Fountain of Youth began to emerge. Alexander the Great reportedly discovered a healing "river of paradise," and archeologists have found similar legends in the Canary Islands, the Caribbean, Japan, and Europe. Most of us learned about Ponce de León and his quest to find the miraculous waters.[1] Humans spend significant amounts of time and money striving to live forever.

In the early 1800s, the American life expectancy was about forty. Over the next hundred years, that number rose only seven years; however, in the last century, that number has risen into the mid to late seventies.[2]

That jump stems from the significant improvements in health care we've seen over the last couple of decades. Doctors can prevent many cardiac events. Scientists find new treatments for cancer every day. We've even seen progress in slowing down dementia and Alzheimer's. With so much additional information at our fingertips about DNA and how the human body works, humans can now live longer than ever.

However, a longer life without the health to go with it is no life at all. This understanding spotlighted the term health span. Men and women want more than just the ability to live to be ninety or a hundred; they want to enjoy and participate in living every day of those ten decades. The internet gives us unlimited access to exercise videos, nutrition advice, and the means to keep our body and mind strong longer than ever before.

Science, technology, and knowledge of nutrition and the human body continue to make rapid progress. Still, there's one vital subject related to longevity people seem to be missing. For instance, say you have the ability to increase your lifespan to reach 100. Will you have enough money to fund your longer life?

Despite the fact we have a chance for an expanded healthful life, the Three Financial Diseases[IP] threaten our chances to live life full and free. Have you entertained the difficult discussions surrounding the things that can rob you of the best future possible?

The Disease of Undisciplined Spending

Emotional eating has become a buzzword today. A web search will give you thousands of articles to help you identify and overcome this weight loss detriment. However, when we begin to talk about the problem of emotional spending or compulsive buying, the availability of information drops considerably. Believe it or not, emotional spending can be as detrimental as emotional eating. When we allow our feelings to drive us, we end up with all kinds of things we don't need and less of the hard-earned money we do need.

Some think this illness only affects those of little means. They are under the impression that the lack of money means the person is being frivolous or undisciplined; however, the wealthy and middle class can easily get caught up in the same game. In fact, the impact of undisciplined spending can be even more devastating in a wealthy family. For example, if a wealthy person decides not to leave any assets for children or charity and instead decides to spend all his resources, he is susceptible to some of the most irrational spending decisions.

The saddest part in these circumstances is that most of these families once displayed the tenets of healthy financial living by being thoughtful, disciplined, and process-driven in whatever business or initiative that made them successful in the first place. In one generation, those positive habits can quickly be replaced by impulsive, erratic buying and investing with no focus on building assets for the future. It may look less devastating in the short run because they can still pay their bills, but the outcome will be the same.

The mindsets that keep us from eating healthy and exercising consistently also compromise our financial future. When we talk about eating, spending, or saving, no one likes to hear the phrase self-control. We've all been tempted by that last tasty morsel in the cookie jar. All day we walk by and resist. Finally, after passing the sugary goodness ten or fifteen times, we give in. In the same way, we talk ourselves into that piece of clothing, electronic gadget, or bigger ticket item.

Do we need it?

As much as we need a cookie.

Humans often rationalize our money away. Sometimes it comes from fear of missing out (FOMO), and other times we're like a fish chasing a shiny lure. When the item we've got our eye on is inexpensive, we tell ourselves, "It's only twenty dollars." And before we know it, we've blown a few hundred or thousand without much to show for it.

The lack of self-discipline is the number one disease eating away at our chances for Financial Longevity[IP]. Schools once taught shop, sewing, and cooking as essential life skills. We've recently seen an emphasis on helping young people understand the importance of physical activity, mental health, and nutritional eating. But for some reason, we avoid any talk of healthy money practices. And like any subject where we have little to no familiarity, training, or education, we become afraid of it or sensationalize it. With the rise of credit cards and other virtual forms of payment, young people don't understand the dangers of overspending. Even adults get lulled into feeling like they never run out of funds.

Unfortunately, these same cards that give you the false sense of security also cost the public hundreds or thousands in interest and fees every year. Interest rates have reached their highest level in over twenty years. This means our ability to pay off these high-interest loans becomes more difficult with each dollar we add to the debt. The Consumer Financial Protection Bureau estimates Americans pay roughly $120 billion each year in credit card interest and fees.[3] And too many of us contribute to that amount. The ease of getting credit, the lack of understanding of how to use it effectively, and the power of compounding interest on these debts put most Americans well behind the eight ball when it comes to creating a healthy financial plan for their future.

Too many adults don't have a handle on how much they should be saving or the most effective ways to save. Marketing gurus thrive on impulse buyers. Social media advertising, store endcaps, and shelf placement all focus on the person who makes purchases based on whims and the power of suggestion. This disease of spending and saving without discipline kills the financial futures of too many each year, and it hits men and women of every economic status. However, unlike physical ailments, the loss goes unreported.

Infected Investment Philosophies

How many times have you seen a workout regimen on TikTok or Instagram and jumped on the bandwagon? The video promises thirty-day abs or the perfect physique by Christmas. Fad diets work the same way. Over the years, we've seen South Beach, Keto, Atkins, Paleo, Master Cleanse, and more. This notion of speedy weight loss has become a seventy-billion-dollar industry, not because it works[4]—if you've tried one of those high-promise programs, you've already figured out the success rate is low—but because Americans have become a society that craves instant gratification.

An investment philosophy based on get-rich-quick strategies works the same way, except it can prove much more catastrophic. We've seen people grab hold of the latest money-making scheme or make an investment and change their minds within a year or two. Despite being told history showed a great ten-year return, impatience causes them to move on to the next great-looking investment. They end up buying and selling, paying extra in fees and taxes, and spinning their wheels to get nowhere.

Without dedication to learning the intricacies of the various forms of investing, the plethora of information on the internet doesn't help. You'll find articles on mutual funds and ETFs, Robo-this and Auto-that. This instant gratification infection steals precious funds from people every day. And unfortunately, because social media allows us to share our misinformation so readily, the disease spreads faster than a cold in a Kindergarten class.

Ailments from External Sources

Some of our health issues can be traced back to our parents and grandparents. Scientists use DNA tests to tell physicians which patients have higher risks of cancer. This gives doctors the ability to screen more frequently and promote early detection.

Sadly, other physically inherited diseases come straight from our environment. Children who grow up on fast food or a high percentage of processed foods usually find themselves struggling with obesity or diabetes. Constant negativity contributes to mental disease. Even a small thing, like not being taught the need for a proper amount of sleep, can cause health problems as we age.

Perhaps you're already thinking about the money lessons you learned as a child. Those who grew up with parents who lived through the Great Depression may have been taught to be extremely frugal and afraid of banks. Some whose parents gave them money any time they asked for it probably weren't aware money didn't grow on trees until they moved out on their own.

We also face physical ailments from other external factors. Broken bones come from hard falls, car accidents create lifelong back problems, pollen and dust make your allergies kick in. In the same way, family and social dynamics can stir up symptoms in your financial world.

Relationships often spur people to make bad decisions—health decisions as well as financial decisions. Think about the last time you had a family disruption. You fought with your siblings, or your children stopped talking to one another. Depression sets in and you try to spend your way out of it.

We've seen parents use money to try to buy their way out of difficult situations. The kid hates their parents because they didn't support their child's harmful life choice. Instead of sticking to their guns, the parents pay the child's bills or go into debt to buy their child a car. This disease might be the deadliest because it reaches other members of the family. They don't get the illness, but they feel the effects. In multi-children families, if a parent bails one adult child out of their self-inflicted problems, the other children suffer when it comes time to divide the inheritance. How is it fair that the son or daughter who took half of the parents' savings while their parents were living also gets a quarter of what's left when the will is read?

Just as bad, when these fifty-, sixty-, and seventy-year-olds should be thinking about slowing down, retiring, traveling, and enjoying everything they worked so hard to save, they don't have enough to support a bigger, better lifestyle. Now, not only does the child suffer because he or she always got a bail out, but siblings also get cheated, and the parents struggle too.

I know one man who graciously decided to personally guarantee an enormous line of credit for his son's business. He's still working well into his seventies because that debt hangs over his head. Another woman I've talked to could be quite comfortable in her retirement years. She wouldn't be wealthy by any means, but she would have plenty—except she's still supporting her middle-aged daughter. The mother makes all the daughter's car payments and pays her rent. Any plans these two older adults had for cruises or spoiling their grandchildren have been redirected. Their Financial Longevity is compromised because of this exogenous disease.

Your Health Span Needs Wealth Span[IP]

If you're like me, you're working toward physical and mental wellness and an increased health span. But that means you'll also need to think about your longer, healthier life from a financial perspective. Most people want a Wealth Span[IP] that lasts as long as their health span.

Regardless, too many have upgraded their medical care from 2.0 to 3.0 while their financial system hasn't been shifted since Windows 95. Most cash flow plans are set up to take a person through eighty-five or ninety if they're lucky. But if the medical community keeps going in the direction they're going now, that won't be enough. A few Dutch scientists anticipate average life expectancy to hit 125 by 2070.[5] In fact, because of the breakthroughs in medical advancement over the last decade, Strategic Coach® co-founder Dan Sullivan has set his sights on 156.[6]

The most important question becomes, "Will you have a Wealth Span—enough money to live comfortably until you die—that will keep up with your health span?"

If you see yourself or someone you love afflicted with any of these diseases, I have good news. Each of these financial curses can be cured. You'll need a change in mindset and a determination to leave behind your bad habits. The advances in medicine and technology offer us huge opportunities to live more years on this planet. However, if you plan to enjoy a lengthier health span, it's vital to be prepared. So, let's take a closer look at understanding the ins and outs of intentionally creating a path to a Wealth Span that will give you vibrant Financial Longevity.

PART TWO
Finance

CHAPTER TWO

It Doesn't Have to Be Complicated

One of the reasons I got into this business was to help simplify things that seem complicated. On Friday evenings while I was in college, I would sit with my grandmother, a Holocaust survivor, and help her make sense of her financial statements. While my father and uncle, both attorneys, had tried to explain her pension and bank reports, she told me I was the only one who made it clear for her. I loved being able to do that for Bubbie, though at the time, I didn't think about applying it to a career.

After college, I moved into the corporate finance world, but as I considered working in wealth management, I remembered what my grandmother had said about me, and I knew I wanted to add that kind of clarity to the lives of others like her.

Many topics in finance seem complicated. But they don't have to be. People also think the more money you have, the more complicated it gets. That's just not true. I thrive on taking the complex and making it simple[IP].

It Does Have to Be Personalized

So, while finances don't have to be complex, they do need to be personalized. Much of our financial picture overlaps the way we develop our health. Children who learn healthy eating habits have a much easier time staying fit than those who develop junk food habits. Likewise, most kids who learn to save will carry those financial lessons with them for the rest of their lives. And just like it takes time and hard work to get in physical shape, being financially fit requires a plan and dedication.

I recently heard a speaker share how Artificial Intelligence (AI) is reshaping medicine. As technology grows, AI will help create new pharmaceuticals to increase longevity, and it will even make our prescriptions more specific—not merely disease-specific but biochemistry-specific. You and I could have the same illness, yet the medications we take will differ according to our DNA as well as our RNA (Ribonucleic Acid—the strings that transport messages to your unique DNA).[7] The term "a good, long life" will be redefined as these personalized plans give people more time and a higher quality of life. You need the same kind of plan for your finances, and it doesn't have to be difficult.

Your financial plan should be as unique as your DNA. But like those medicines they'll be creating to accommodate our different biochemistries, every Financial Longevity plan begins with some basic similarities. Everyone should start with the Four Financial Priorities[IP], and they fall in this chronological order.

1. **Get rid of high-interest debt** – Any loan that doesn't provide some tax advantage will rob you. Mortgages and student loans sometimes offer deductions that offset the interest you pay. But credit cards and unsecured loans can eat away at your healthy balance sheet and cash flow like a cancer. They inhibit your ability to live free.

   Yes, the plan looks a bit different depending on where you start from. Some will have only a thousand or two in debt to whittle down, while others have several cards maxed out. However, the first priority means eradicating these obligations.
2. **Create an Emergency Fund** – Some call this a rainy-day fund. Whatever term you use, after those high-interest debts have been wiped out, it's time to put funds back to cover the unexpected. What will you do if you lose your job or have a medical emergency? How will you pay to repair your house if the washer floods the laundry room? If you don't have a plan, these unforeseen expenses will end up on your credit card, adding to this most aggressive form of debt.

   We recommend having enough in your Emergency Fund to cover three to six months of expenses—both fixed and variable. Fixed expenses include your housing, food, and transportation costs, as well as any loans you're still paying. Entertainment, shopping, and vacations fall in the Variable category. Look at your bank statements or the amount of cash you spend each month on these discretionary items and add a median amount to your fixed expenses. Then multiply by six to determine how much you need in a savings account in case of emergency. Hopefully, you're reading this book before you've put yourself into debt because that means you can quickly build this second priority and move right into number three.

3. **Savings** – After you've built up your rainy-day fund, you can put back a bit each month in a more discretionary savings account. This gives you the flexibility to avoid unnecessary loans and credit cards because you have these funds to cover your disciplined expenses. In today's banking environment, you can earn a very healthy interest rate on your savings, so shop around and compare rates on savings accounts at different banks. A four percent interest rate on $1,000 in your savings account can add $40 annually to your coffers. In an ideal world, numbers three and four of this list can be built together.
4. **Investments** – Investing is the fun part of your financial plan. It's best done with an advisor who knows his or her way around this realm of the finance industry and is focused on providing guidance in their client's best interest. And again, because your situation will not be exactly like anyone else's, a great advisor will talk to you about your short-term, medium-term, and long-term goals.

One of the easiest and most effective forms of investing is making sure you're taking advantage of any match your employer offers for a 401k. If they will match up to three percent, then three percent needs to be your minimum payroll deduction.

For most, long-term goals are easy—retirement and legacy giving. On the other hand, a short-term goal for some is a new car every three years, while others want to plan a grand vacation every summer. Medium-term goals might include a downpayment on a house or a college fund for your children. Investing allows you to reach these milestones more quickly than a basic savings account.

It's important to begin building these priorities as early as possible. The crux of the plan is to spend less than you make and live beneath your means. However, just like you need a physician to personalize your health span, if you want to maximize your Wealth Span, you will need to lean on a wealth advisor who knows you and your goals to walk you through your financial decisions.

It Does Have to Be Comprehensive

Everyone agrees we need a comprehensive health plan. No one would limit their physician visits to a podiatrist. We want our doctor to check our heart, lungs, skin, brain, and more. Additionally, when our health needs get more complex, our primary physician will often refer us to a specialist to give us a more comprehensive plan for recovery.

Unfortunately, many think only high-net-worth individuals need that same kind of detailed financial picture. But that couldn't be further from the truth. If you want a Wealth Span that offers Financial Longevity, you need a personalized plan including all the pieces a family office offers those with significant wealth.

A comprehensive plan begins by meeting with an advisor who digs into your current financial situation and your goals. The discovery call, as well as subsequent conversations, may prove to be the most important aspect of your plan.

"Do you want to buy a house?"

"When will you need a new car?"

"Are you currently between jobs? Do you need cash flow until you begin your new position?"

"Are you about to start a family or embark on a new career?

"When would you like to retire or begin to work a little less so you can enjoy life a little more?"

All these questions and more set the stage for the way your advisor will move ahead, modeling a few future scenarios for you to choose from. I'm a visual learner, so I enjoy creating images to help my clients envision their next few decades. These conversations set the stage for the rest of the relationship and prepare us to give you the best advice for Financial Longevity.

Think about how difficult it would be to get your dream house built if you never sat down with the architect and gave her all the details. How will she know you want a wall of windows leading onto the back deck or skylights in the loft? You can't get the perfect design if you don't have meaningful conversations with the person who is creating the plan for your future. And just like the conversations continue throughout the building process when you hire an architect, the conversation with your advisor should be ongoing. Every life change requires a discussion so adjustments can be as effective as possible.

A comprehensive plan brings tax and estate planners into the picture. While your wealth advisor will manage your plan, these other key individuals will help shape the plan so it takes advantage of current laws and allows you to leave a legacy.

Your advisor looks at assets, cash flow, charitable giving, and insurance needs to put together a three-fold plan to help you live your best life in the present and the future. Most importantly, your plan should be one you understand.

As you look for an advisor, you'll want to be sure to engage someone who believes creating your plan is as important as the plans set up for the Vanguards or the Rockefellers. Ideally, interviewing several advisors before making a choice is ideal. This allows you to be sure you've got a good fit from both a relationship and expertise standpoint. When interviewing an advisor, ask about their experience, the services they offer, their investment philosophy (we'll talk more about this later in the book), how often they plan to communicate with you, and their approach to financial planning. Also, make sure you understand how the advisor gets paid, as there are several pricing models in the industry. You should also find out if the advisor acts as a fiduciary, which implies that they must put your best interests before their own.

Unfortunately, it doesn't matter how well we plan if we haven't put up safeguards against those three deadly diseases.

CHAPTER THREE

Curing the Disease of Being Undisciplined

When we think of discipline, our thoughts automatically go negative. We envision running suicides at basketball practice or Dad grounding us for two months. Often, we label those lessons from our parents or coaches as punishment; however, discipline and punishment are two very different things.

Punishment is a negative consequence of our bad behavior, while discipline is the creation of good habits resulting in positivity and growth. Yes, parents often use punishment to teach a six-year-old discipline. Hopefully, the older we get, the more we see the value in developing discipline prior to the punishment.

In our health span, lack of discipline looks like heart disease unchecked or a diabetic who chooses to eat cake after every meal despite the fact their glucose level is over three hundred. And in those cases, the consequences can be deadly. Refusing to develop some serious discipline in our financial life can create something that feels almost as tragic. The thought of running out of money can create a feeling of panic similar to the fear we feel when threatened with a serious health challenge.

Start Early

The number one tip I give people to help them develop discipline is to start early. By four, children begin to understand they can't have cookies before dinner and they need to eat their vegetables in order to have dessert. Most families want their children to have a well-balanced diet and good eating habits. Unfortunately, fewer teach the importance of well-balanced spending and saving habits.

Parents who teach their children to save a percentage of their allowance or put back a bit of their birthday money give them a phenomenal gift. When you help teens understand that either they control their credit cards or their credit cards control them, you set them on the road to success. It's much easier to put a habit of saving and disciplined spending in place when you don't have other financial burdens like rent or utilities.

But what if you didn't learn to save or control your spending as a child? It's never too late to start. The key is remembering that good financial habits, like any other habit-creating exercise, take time and don't happen quickly. Most people quit dieting because they only lose one pound a week and won't wait for the cumulative results. The same goes for financial habits. Compounding your savings takes time. Be patient. Modify your plan when necessary, but whatever you do, never quit.

Start with those First Four Financial Priorities I mentioned in the last chapter. Take control of your credit cards and learn to differentiate between discretionary wants and actual needs. Then you can begin to save. No amount is too small. One hundred dollars a year works out to less than nine dollars a month, and while it seems slow, it's the beginning of an important habit. Gradually, as your income increases and you develop more discipline, you can increase the amount you put back each month.

Regardless of the amount you save, timing is everything. Every month you wait to begin creating discipline in your life is one month of out-of-control spending that will add to your debt and subtract from your Financial Longevity.

Understand Credit and Debit Cards

More than eighty percent of American adults have a credit card, and an additional ten percent also have at least one debit card.[8] Twenty-year-olds carry about two credit cards, while older Americans average about four.[9] Ease of use, online shopping, and various rewards have made plastic and virtual cards more and more popular.

Sadly, too many people don't understand the differences or risks involved in using these electronic funds. Both fall prey to fraud and both require vigilance when we use them. Unlike cash, which makes it easy to identify when funds are running low, the convenience of these cards means we can overdraw our bank account or spend more than we should without thinking about it.

Because credit cards are so easy to use, their balances end up growing without us noticing. Plus, interest charges and fees can add to what we owe if we aren't careful. In order to control the card rather than having it control you, we need to take it to a zero balance with every statement.

On the other hand, we don't have to worry about paying off debit cards every month. The money comes straight from our bank account. This also means we never have to worry about interest. Yet debit cards have a downside as well. They don't help our credit rating like credit cards can, and since they're attached to our cash account, if fraudulent charges hit, we feel it exponentially.

Cash is an excellent third option for spending—especially for those trying to develop more discipline. Because we can touch it, we're more careful with it. And it's impossible to spend more cash than we have.

Cash is the root of a very effective money management method called envelope system budgeting. To implement, you allocate specific amounts of money to different spending categories. Each payday, you put your allocations in separate envelopes and never spend more than the contents until the next payday. This helps control spending and ensures you don't overspend in any category. The recent trend to phase out cash is beginning to challenge this otherwise effective beginning budgeting strategy. Don't fear; there is an app for that! Goodbudget allows users to implement the envelope system digitally.

Controlling Impulses

Impulse buying can be as difficult to control as emotional eating. Perhaps you're a chronic shop at home junkie (e.g., QVC or HSN). You love buying knives in the middle of the night. You wonder, "How can I keep from doing that? I mean, I can stop for a while, but eventually, the itch gets too bad."

Some people might need the help of a counselor. Something deep within, a memory from the past perhaps, triggers the urge, and professional help is the only cure. Others might simply be able to turn off the TV or remove an app from their phone. You can even set up controls on your computer that block sites so you won't be tempted to visit.

People have resorted to putting their credit cards in a glass of water in the freezer to force them to think about their purchases, and a few make sure they never go to the store alone. They have given a trusted friend permission to hold them accountable.

Unfortunately, depending on your personality, it might be impossible to completely rid yourself of this impulse to shop. That level of rigidity might not be realistic for you.

In that case, I recommend setting up a slush fund. Calculate the amount you can afford to set aside each payday—an amount that won't take you off the path of your plan—and add it to your slush fund. However, you only get to add to the slush fund when you've successfully reached your savings goals. If you don't maintain discipline in reaching those milestones, the slush fund isn't replenished. But if you have managed to create a sustainable savings discipline, on those occasions when you can't help yourself, you can dip into your slush account to take the edge off the itch as a reward.

As you grow accustomed to waiting for the slush fund to grow, you also begin to break the habit of impulse spending. Before you know it, you might actually start spending the slush fund on smart things—splurge items you'll actually use.

However, understanding your credit and debit cards and getting your impulse buying under control is only the first step in curing the disease of undisciplined finances.

CHAPTER FOUR

Slow and Steady Wins the Race

Imagine planting a seed and then going out to the spot where you planted it day after day with water and fertilizer with nothing to show for your diligence. How long would you show up to that patch of dirt before you gave up? In this fast-paced world we live in, when results don't appear immediately, most humans change course or quit altogether.

The Chinese Bamboo Tree is famous for being the slowest growing tree in the world. The seed requires daily water and fertilizer for five years. If the farmer misses even one day, the tree will never break through. By the time the first bit of green pops out of the dirt, the farmer has developed quite a habit. But then, almost miraculously, the seed turns into something marvelous. In just six weeks, a ninety-foot giant stands on that spot of dirt. But without the farmer's small gesture for 1,826 days, he would never have experienced its beauty.

One Percent

In his book *Atomic Habits*, James Clear asserts if you can improve yourself by just one percent every day for one year, at the end of the year, you'll be thirty-seven times better. Imagine how much a person's health could improve if they made one small change every week. Week one they switch from mayonnaise to mustard or hummus. Week two, they swap out their creamer for 2 percent milk. Week three takes sugary or carbonated drinks to water.[10] Small diet changes have proven to have a great impact over time.[11] Many people who count calories or go on a meal plan aren't satisfied with the small changes. For instance, a person loses two pounds in a week, but he doesn't think it's enough. After two weeks of such a seemingly insignificant change, he gives up. People like this dismiss their progress. To succeed, we have to be okay with a one percent change. We have to see each small change as a step forward and keep going despite the fact it looks so minuscule.

Learning financial discipline doesn't happen any faster than healthy eating habits. They happen one small move at a time. The slow pace will frustrate you. Think about how despondent our farmer felt after four hundred days of watering a patch of dirt with no sign of success. Yep, that's how it will feel sometimes.

It's important to remember every drop of water the farmer carried to the tree brought growth. Even when he couldn't see it happening, the tree was getting bigger. Just because we can't see the change, every effort takes us a step in the right direction. Chasing the one percent is how you change habits.

Suppose you take just one percent of your paycheck each month and put it in savings. Even the person who makes only $24,000 each year will have $240 in their account after twelve months. However, if this same person increased their deposit by one percent a month, the amount at the end of the year grows to $1,560. I know it still seems like so little; however, if you continued to save that amount for twenty years and earned seven percent on those deposits, you would have just under $64,000!

With every pay raise or promotion, you have the power to increase your deposit. And every step of added discipline allows you to up your monthly contribution. The point of the exercise is more than simply accumulating money. Your consistency creates a habit. You develop discipline. By accepting the one percent challenge, you increase your level of success, and the new habit you curate will also boost your self-confidence.

Pay Yourself

You've probably already disciplined yourself in some aspects of your finances. Every month, you pay your mortgage or rent, utility, and cell phone bills. Most Americans understand these are absolute necessities, and anyone with a shred of responsibility makes sure each one arrives at their respective offices on time.

Many people have other loans or obligations they pay every month. Car payments, streaming services, and WiFi are just a few of the less necessary bills we make sure get paid regularly. If we want Financial Longevity and a Wealth Span that outlasts our health span, we simply must elevate our savings account to the same level of importance as our electric bill.

Whether you deposit ten dollars each payday or one hundred, it's time to recognize the magnitude of your decision to build that emergency fund. Setting this as a priority is an investment in yourself and your future.

James Clear says it like this: "Every action you take is a vote for the type of person you wish to become."[12] "All big things come from small beginnings. The seed of every habit is a single, tiny decision. But as that decision is repeated, a habit sprouts and grows stronger. Roots entrench themselves and branches grow."[13]

As you begin the journey to Financial Longevity, take a moment to look at your long-term goals and break them down into small chunks. If you have more than ten years left to grow your Wealth Span, you might split your growth years in anticipation of a bigger paycheck as you get promoted. For example, you might plan to accumulate thirty percent of our total plan during the first five years and seventy percent during the final years. Remember, your process must be personalized. And customizing it into achievable phases will set you up for success.

CHAPTER FIVE

Not One and Done

Imagine visiting the doctor on your thirtieth birthday then never returning because you got a clean bill of health. Many things can change between the ages of thirty and sixty. The American Medical Association recommends visiting your primary care physician every two or three years until you turn fifty, and then annually. Most health professionals recognize that regular checkups are a must.[14] Even if you're feeling well and have a clean bill of health, you probably need advice on what to eat because calorie and nutrition requirements change as we age. To secure an increased health span, we need periodic evaluations, and our finances are no different.

Evaluate and Reevaluate

The third step in creating a highly disciplined lifestyle that will produce the Wealth Span you need is to constantly revisit your plan. Whether you're in the Priority One Phase paying off your debt or you've been investing for sixty years, you need to step back and reevaluate your methods on a regular basis.

When our journey toward Financial Longevity starts extremely small, we often think we don't need an annual review. How can the little we contribute to our savings or investments create a scenario where we need to evaluate our plan? Isn't it too small to matter? But consider how dangerous it would be if your physician didn't take your blood pressure regularly, or if diabetics refused to monitor their glucose levels.

Focusing on one percent will mean we often won't notice the significance of the slight changes in our behavior and finances. The review process for your finances will show you that no amount is too small. You'll be able to see where you've improved and be encouraged to set new goals. Whether you make this a monthly, quarterly, or annual evaluation, only a deep review into where we've been and how far we've come will allow us to see our success.

Push the Limits

Recognizing our accomplishments lets us step up our plan to reach our goals even sooner. But that can only happen if you're willing to consistently push a bit harder. When you achieve a milestone or notice you're keeping up with the class, it's time to move ahead. Revisiting your goals and progress might reveal it's time to increase your 401K deposits or start a Roth IRA.

Every time you move to the next level, it will feel hard to keep up for a while, but the more you stick with your plan, the easier it becomes to go a little further. You become like a runner training for a marathon. They begin with a mile or two a day and gradually increase their distance. Anytime their run becomes too easy, they push themselves to go farther until they can complete the twenty-six miles with ease.

That's the idea behind these regular reviews. When saving fifty dollars a month gets comfortable, ask yourself, "Can I push a little further?" Taking that fifty dollars to seventy-five might hurt for a while. But because you've seen positive results before, you'll be motivated to keep going forward.

If you have the slush fund I mentioned earlier, this annual review becomes the perfect time to see how you're doing with your impulse spending. After a couple years of small steps, you may discover you've become even more disciplined. When you get to that place where you almost never touch this "permission to spend" account, it's probably time to redirect at least some of that money to grow your savings or investments. But how will you know without an evaluation?

The Four Financial Priorities give evidence that we can't rest on our laurels simply because we've gotten a good start. After you develop discipline to pay off your debt and progress in your savings, it's time to move into investing. Your evaluation will help you determine the appropriate time, but do you know everything you need to know about this phase of Financial Longevity?

CHAPTER SIX

Upgrading Your Investment Philosophy

As you move into the investment phase of the Four Priorities, you'll find a number of philosophies and theories, and most include a modicum of truth and realism. Meme stocks and cryptocurrency can sound very logical, but we need more than a modicum of logic when we're investing.

Despite the variety of opinions, you'll find a few tenets most reputable advisors agree on. These include a three-fold plan that is the most tried and true way to create wealth through investing—invest in quality assets, own them for a long time, and ride them through the ups and downs.

Buy Quality

In the medical world, many companies tout supplements. Vitamins, minerals, diet pills, physical enhancement and body-building drugs, sleep aids, and more now number in the tens of thousands. Unfortunately, because the industry has blown up to over $151 billion each year, not all can be trusted. Though some of these supplements offer real, positive results, others have as much potency as a sugar pill, and in a worst-case scenario, they cause adverse health effects.[15]

Achieving good investment results, like knowing which supplements to take, requires significant study and serious work. Quality is key, and finding the right stocks or funds is a lot harder than most people think. To achieve superior performance, it's crucial to do something different than the majority.

Many focus on the latest investment style or trend. However, those who own strong investments—ones that bring solid and repeatable returns—have dug deep and found the highest-quality investments possible. That is a timeless strategy.

I believe that owning high-quality assets is the best way to achieve strong risk-adjusted returns over long periods of time. We also believe that when you find a high-quality business, you have to invest enough in that company so that its performance has a positive impact on your bottom line. Owning larger stakes in fewer high-quality assets—otherwise known as concentrated investing—ensures that as the cream rises to the top, your investment portfolio will see big benefits. Owning fewer quality holdings also protects against a negative surprise, like unfamiliar holdings foiling your performance.

We recently reviewed a fixed-income mutual fund that had over three thousand holdings. I got dizzy just thinking about how anyone could truly monitor and understand that many offerings. Most investors constantly shift allocations and chase the "hot dot." They hire and fire mutual fund managers and trade in and out of funds based on trends, never holding an investment or following an investment philosophy long enough to let time and compounding work their magic. Worse still, most mutual funds underperform their benchmarks, according to CNBC and Morningstar, so in many cases, novice investors are just churning from one underperformer to another, creating unnecessary transactions and potentially higher fees.[16]

Unfortunately, there are nearly as many low-quality investments as there are useless or harmful supplements. It helps when you know what to watch out for.

Beware of Meme Stocks

When we're looking for quality stocks, we have to remember to avoid the "too good to be true" list. These fads flood social media on a regular basis, and they look like easy ways to make money. Meme stocks, as these internet fads are called, have become popular among amateur investors, but like all these flashes in the pan, they will knock you off your plan.

How can you tell if the investment you're thinking about is a fad? One good indicator is how you feel physically when you think about it. If your heart starts pumping fast and you find yourself with a bit of FOMO or feel like you're behind the eight ball, that investment is probably a fad.

Quality investments will give you a more confident feeling. You have more control over your emotions. When your emotions trump logic and fundamentals, you'll know you are potentially heading into trouble.

Fads tend to convince us to abandon discipline and persuade us to justify our actions. If you're afraid to tell people you're buying into a stock because of what they'll say, it's probably a bad idea. Yes, sometimes you'll make a little money on those fads, but that's just good fortune. It's not the result of putting in the work and sticking to your discipline.

We've all had those friends who, despite the fact they ate fast food and donuts all through high school and college, excelled at sports and never gained weight. Fast forward thirty years and those same people don't look like that anymore. In fact, they have all kinds of health issues brought on by a poor diet. Yes, it worked for them for a while, but the processed food diet just isn't sustainable.

The r/WallStreetBets (WSB) community on Reddit gave us a good example of social media's fantasy advice. In 2021, WSB's amateur investor community exorbitantly pushed up the stock price for GameStop, though the future of the company itself was in question. Hedge funds were short-selling the stock, but WSB kept driving the price up. Unfortunately, while the SEC requires advisors to vet hedge fund investors—they must have enough net worth that any loss will not put them in financial distress—WSB amateurs had no such protection. At least one young man committed suicide after a perceived loss of $730,000.[17]

There are any number of these fun-looking investments, but nothing will top buying into top-producing businesses with a track record and high productivity. If you come across an investment opportunity that seems too good to be true or something social media boasts about, you should consult a wealth advisor before you part with your hard-earned funds. Always remember, if it looks too good to be true, it usually is.

Investing in Cryptocurrency

Bitcoin and other cryptocurrencies have also caught the attention of many investors. And while there are definitely some advantages to the idea of digital currency, this decentralized funding source is also still unregulated. The Bitcoin website boasts their unregulated status as an advantage over other currencies. But that's why it has become the payment method of choice for cybercrime.

The code that creates Bitcoin on Blockchain, the public ledger that verifies and records the cryptocurrency, has been set to limit the number of Bitcoin to twenty-one million. This cap has historically kept the price on an upward trend. Anton Mozgovoy, co-founder and CEO of Holyheld, a digital financial service company, says Bitcoin is worth money "simply because we, as people, decided it has value—same as gold."[18]

However, I believe the current lack of regulation, the volatility, and the fact cryptocurrency is currency-like—comparable to gold—take it out of the quality investment category. I will say that separate from cryptocurrency, blockchain technology is very exciting and could be a preferred method of clearing financial transactions in the future. Also, there is increased chatter after the 2024 U.S. Presidential Election about regulating cryptocurrency and even creating a digital dollar, developments that could change the utilization of crypto in the future.

Every fad has a bubble—a short period of time where the rising price will tempt you to buy in. GameStop had its bubble, and we've seen real estate bubbles. They look good, and the promises they make have the potential to trip you up. Discipline will be your only friend if you feel like you just have to get in on one of these too-good-to-be-true investments. The only way to keep from going broke is limiting yourself to only buying an amount that will not throw your plan out the window. You might get in and out at just the right time; however, these bubbles are not sustainable.

"Data shows that owning financially superior and competitively advantaged businesses can offer a margin of safety in almost any market."[19] Characteristics like earnings power, financial stability, and competitive moats allow companies to weather tougher times and power through a crisis faster and stronger than their competitors. Creating a disciplined portfolio focused on the highest-performing businesses in the world gives your investments the potential to be well-positioned to deliver sustainable, above-average earnings for the long haul.[20] Plus, these companies offer an opportunity for resilience during the downturns.

Jack of all trades but master of none is an old adage, but it has a great deal of truth attached to it. In their book *The One Thing*, Gary Keller and Jay Papasan share their theory that to achieve extraordinary business results, you must master a single task and repeat it. They emphasize the beauty of learning to do one thing and doing it with excellence. Few who try to do their own investing have the time or experience to find quality investments. Bringing together a quality portfolio can be difficult, if not impossible, on your own.

Warren Buffett says that nothing creates and maintains wealth better than the ownership of a great business. It's vital to find a team of advisors who have dedicated themselves to finding these kinds of profitable companies if you want a high-quality portfolio that will increase your Wealth Span.

CHAPTER SEVEN

Non-Negotiable Investing

Any bodybuilder will tell you adding muscle requires work. Even if you manage to shed the pounds, you'll need weights or resistance bands to get some definition in those biceps or abs. And even more than that—you're going to have to commit to your workout plan for years. Suppose you do develop great biceps; if you drop your workout plan, they'll fade. Regardless of the promises we hear in those thirty-second reels on Instagram and TikTok, thirty-day abs are a myth.

It Takes Time

The story of the Chinese Bamboo Tree is effective when you move into investing as well. Investments can be a risky thing, and you'll find all kinds of different theories out there about when to invest and the best funds to invest in. However, despite those differences, most advisors and professional investors agree time is the investor's best friend.

Since its inception in 1957, the S&P has had an average annual return of around ten percent. Granted, every ten years or so, the index drops in the negative. But even with those down years figured in, these ever-shifting top five hundred stocks have a history of increasing in value.[21]

What would happen if you invested as little as $100 in one of the S&P Index funds? For illustrative purposes, I like to use 7 percent as a guide when I make projections to keep the numbers conservative. If you added only $100 to your investment every year—less than ten dollars a month—for five years, at the end of that five-year period, you'd have about $610—$110 more than you invested. If you kept doing that for five more years, you would have $1,485. Add another five years, and your money will have nearly doubled, thanks to the principle of compounding interest. Investing $1500 over fifteen years adds more than $1200 in interest to your account, a total of $2728.

You can double that number by making your annual deposit just $200. And if you increase your deposits to $1,000 annually—about $85 a month—you can multiply your total by ten. For as little as $3 a day for fifteen years, the patient investor will see a gain of more than $12,000.

Bear markets (bad markets) have historically been temporary. Share prices typically turn upward twelve months before the bottom of the business cycle. Long-term investors recognize they have only one objective: to maximize total risk-adjusted real returns after taxes.

It Requires Commitment

This idea of giving investments time to grow slowly becomes difficult when we see big fluctuations in the market. Too many see a decline in the index and immediately want to jump ship. Others trust the philosophy of apps and websites instead of dedicating themselves to their plan.

James Clear says, "The purpose of setting goals is to win the game. The purpose of building systems is to continue playing the game. True long-term thinking is goal-less thinking. It's not about any single accomplishment. It is about the cycle of endless refinement and continuous improvement. Ultimately, it is your commitment to the process that will determine your progress."[22]

Committing to an investment plan is crucial to growing real wealth. When we move from Priority Three to Priority Four, we need to carry with us the philosophy and dedication we learned when we started paying ourselves. Those who truly want Financial Longevity must believe in and commit to the plan.

Many social and political issues affect the market, and too often people react to these shifts. Wars, elections, trade conflicts, government upheaval, and more play a role in market fluctuations. I have ridden the waves of change many times, and rarely has it been the right decision to make significant portfolio changes because of macroeconomic issues. Headlines like "markets in turmoil" or "stocks in freefall" can also raise a novice investor's temperature when conditions become challenging. These alarming headlines can challenge the resolve of any investor, regardless of age or experience. The ability to separate signals that should be acted on—fundamental factors like changes in inflation, interest rates, or corporate earnings growth—from the noise we hear every day on the news is an essential element of any successful investment plan.

An advisor you trust can help when that stock ticker on your computer begins to scare you. Indexes or quantitative screens can't help you when markets are down and you're afraid your hard-earned nest egg is at risk. A qualified advisor will help you keep these volatile moments in context and keep you focused on the long-term plan rather than the short-term pain. It is often said that wealth advisors add the most value during these tumultuous times because they help their clients avoid short-term mistakes that will have long-term consequences. This type of consultation can increase your confidence and your ability to stay committed to your long-term plan.

We spend a significant amount of time researching and studying companies to find those with the most potential to provide consistent, long-term growth. Whether your investment plan includes owning individual companies or a high-quality set of funds, we find that many investors leave money on the table by focusing on short-term outcomes.

Those who have the intestinal fortitude to remain committed whether markets are up or down generally see excellent results. When things aren't going well, you can't scrap the plan. In fact, in the most sophisticated cases, when the market isn't performing well, people double down on their plan.

I have clients who are extremely structured. Every month, they invest a set amount in their plans. However, in months when the markets drop considerably, they double their deposits. Many have been doing that for fifteen years because they understand that the market will eventually come back, and they have seen the results of staying consistent, which is another common tenet of successful investment plans.

If you invest in quality things and realize that those stocks are going to do well over long periods of time, this doubling down strategy can prove tremendously valuable.

The real key to growth is making a commitment to adding to your investment plan as regularly as you pay your insurance or car payment. If a diabetic friend doesn't take his insulin because he can't afford it, or an aunt with a serious auto-immune disease skips her medication because she isn't committed to the treatment, we would be mortified. We'd probably be angry to hear the excuses doctors typically hear. "I didn't have time." "I forgot." "I worked late." "I didn't put it on my schedule." How many similarly absurd justifications do we use in our wealth-building?

It's easy to blame fear or a lackadaisical attitude for skipping a scheduled addition to our investments. We get scared during those months when unexpected expenses pop up, but that's what we built the emergency fund for. Our investment plans have to be as contractual as any other obligation we pay each month.

Building assets is perhaps a life-time endeavor, and keeping a long-term focus is one of the hardest things to do in today's investment environment. No qualification for success in investing is more important than a firm mind. Investigating thoroughly and intelligently and making sure you have quality investments allows the investor to remain unswayed by every breeze. The soundness and progressiveness of their overall portfolio holdings will help them remain resolute and calm in periods of great uncertainty, which will likely lead to the most favorable lifetime returns.

It Takes Sacrifice

Every person who has successfully turned their health around understands the need for sacrifice. They spend hours at the gym, on their bikes, or at the trail. Other sacrifices include a change in eating habits. In the quest for a longer health span, people give up processed foods, caffeine, and excess sugar and fats. Diabetics watch carbs, and celiac patients abandon their favorite wheat products. It takes this same determination to have a long Wealth Span.

We enjoy many things on a weekly basis that aren't necessary, some of which might not be good for us. As we grow in our discipline, we learn to sacrifice fancy coffees and extra Amazon spending. Each purchase we forgo gives us that much more to add to our investments. If we add up the amount we spend on frivolous things each month, we might find we have an extra hundred dollars or more to add to our portfolios. These small sacrifices can give us big rewards later.

Whether you opt for a smaller car payment or fewer lattes, when you add time and commitment to your sacrifice, you'll be amazed at the return you'll reap when you're ready to retire.

CHAPTER EIGHT

The Most Dangerous Disease

We meet people all the time who are tremendously disciplined and follow every piece of our investment advice. They have been sacrificing since they graduated from college, patiently waiting for their money to grow, and all their hard work paid off. These ideal clients typically have one weakness—their children.

We all want our children to have a life better than ours. And after working so hard, many well-disciplined individuals do what they can so their children don't have to scrape by like they did. But this kind of philosophy often breeds disease, and their well-meaning sentiments don't teach their children the skills they need to succeed. And though they are missing the warning label you find on cigarettes or artificial sweeteners, the financial illnesses that come with family friction pose the most danger.

The Root of the Disease

Before we can completely diagnose the family component of our financial outlook, we have to honestly look at how we view money. In his book *The Psychology of Money*, Morgan Housel addresses the way personal experiences influence our instincts regarding money.

- Do you see money as a dirty thing?
- A good thing?
- A bad thing?
- An aspirational thing?
- Something you take for granted?

Understanding yourself and your view of finances is invaluable. I recommend Housel's book to everyone embarking on their educational journey. It will help you see how you frame your perception of the subject and give you strategies based on your view. It will also give you an idea of how to best move forward with your educational plan.

In my family, money was posited as a tool. There was nothing joyful about it. Phrases like "money doesn't grow on trees" were common. Money was something we needed—a finite resource. We had enough to buy most things, but not without discipline. I sometimes envied those who could just spend without consciousness because our family seriously considered every purchase.

My dad's law partner, whom I considered a mentor of sorts, sat on the other end of the spectrum. One of his favorite lines was, "Never let your income interfere with your standard of living." I found his relationship with money odd and awe inspiring. He went about happy-go-lucky and carefree while I remember vividly sitting with my dad at his desk on a weekly basis learning how to balance a checkbook.

I learned important lessons from both men, and they shaped the way I view finances. Everyone's perspective has been colored by some person or event surrounding money. It may be a memory of something you experienced when you were very young. I think recognizing that and understanding where you're starting from is important as you head down the path toward Financial Longevity.

No Such Thing as Failure

I've been reading a great deal about longevity and wellness lately. This includes many autobiographies of successful business people, and they share a common thread I believe needs repeating—there is no such thing as failure. Every time we make a mistake, we learn something. Getting it wrong helps us discover ways to do things better or figure out what not to do the next time. We shouldn't fear failure.

Those retiring today make up one of the wealthiest generations in history. But this tremendous blessing has a sad byproduct. This well-off generation forgets to let their children fail. They love helping their kids in a way their parents weren't able to help them. Parents will often reroute their lives so their children can avoid facing adversity. But the raw truth is while it may seem like help in the short run, continually shielding your children from hardship hurts them in the long run.

Without the opportunity to mess it up, the next generation never learns to problem solve. They can't develop the skills necessary to put the pieces of their lives together, and they more easily fall into the trap of the first two diseases.

After struggling in grade school and high school because their parents didn't make them work for grades, they flounder through college or drop out. Their peers with parents who held back on their finances and forced them to work for grades and get a job in their teens fly past them in the job market. And with each failure, Mom and Dad remove the obstacle. In the worst cases, these underachievers pass their bad habits along to another generation. All because someone saw struggling and failing as a bad thing.

Each mishap your child faces holds a valuable lesson. Consider all the knowledge you gained from your hard work and the things that went wrong. We have to be willing to allow our children to fail along the way so they learn hard work, perseverance, and the lesson of picking themselves up and starting over again.

Give Them Real Help

I realize for some, it's impossible not to continually bail out your kids. Your personality just won't allow you to let your child fall. More than one couple has risked their retirement or worked till age eighty because their thirty-five-year-old son never developed a work ethic or spends his money on things other than his rent. Mom and Dad feel the need to pay his bills so he doesn't end up on the street.

In a family with several children, the malady usually hits only one or two. But this means the other siblings are being robbed of their inheritance. Every penny you spend on your undisciplined child takes away your ability to enjoy a comfortable retirement and also dips into your legacy giving.

If you refuse to let your child fall, at least protect your offspring who are standing on their own and the charities you want to support after you're gone. You can craft a plan to reward your disciplined heirs as well as help your wayward child face some consequences while you continue to bail them out.

First, you'll need to create a ledger to track the expenses you're covering. Then, make it clear to your son or daughter that the amount on that spreadsheet will be deducted from what they receive after you're gone. This decision will require a change in your will and keeping your estate planner up to date on that ledger; however, the time you invest will be worth so much more.

Sometimes, the problem is greater than merely financial discipline. Nearly thirty percent of American families deal with some form of drug abuse,[23] and about one in twenty-five adults struggle with severe mental health issues.[24] In these cases, parents feel like they have no choice but to help their floundering child, and rightly so. But too often, in an effort to save money, the family avoids bringing in professionals. Sadly, by the time they pay the child's bills and ride the emotional roller coaster, being the superhero actually costs more than hiring experts.

Because these counselors and psychiatrists deal with these issues every day, recovery time can often be faster, and better yet, relationships begin to heal. In my experience, writing a check to the professional rather than the electric company actually relieves much of the financial strain and helps improve the entire family's mental health.

Whether your child needs to learn financial responsibility or needs medical attention, the message you send to your children by taking positive action will prove invaluable. Your responsible children will feel appreciated, and you'll alleviate any resentment that might be brewing. Your sick children will develop coping strategies, and hopefully, when the irresponsible child begins to see his choices have consequences—that he will ultimately have to make some sacrifices—he will begin to turn himself around so by the time the attorney reads your will, he can stand on his own. Otherwise, you leave him very vulnerable after you're gone and your other children in a potentially burdensome position.

Fortunately, there is tremendous help for this exogenous financial disease, and it can be as simple as gathering everyone together for a family meal.

CHAPTER NINE

Communication is Key

Most of these exogenous factors have a common root—lack of communication. Families don't usually talk about money or health issues. Just thinking about the discussion causes anxiety and friction. Parents often don't want to let even their adult children into that part of their world. They don't want to worry their children with problems, and if they never learned how to have that kind of conversation when they were young, they unwittingly spread the disease.

My grandmother's generation fell into that category. When those men and women born during or just after the Great Depression died, you had no idea if they were penniless, in debt, or had two hundred million dollars in a portfolio. They didn't talk about it, and they didn't enjoy spending it.

Create Candid Conversations

Unfortunately, this lack of knowledge leaves some children with a false impression of their parents' financial capability.

Without these candid conversations, even responsible children with the best of intentions may ask their parents to help when finances get tight. For instance, it's typical to ask parents to guarantee a first car loan or mortgage. Without the aid of communication, the children may have no idea the strain that signature could potentially put on their parents' budget, credit rating, or retirement plans, not to mention the stress it may add to a parent's life at a time they are supposed to be enjoying the fruits of their labor.

On the other hand, families who've tackled these tough topics give their children critical information and an opportunity to surprise them. When my mom told me she had a rare blood cancer, I think she was just as concerned about protecting my feelings as she was about her mortality. When our children become adults, we have to remember that while they will always be our kids, some may have talents, skills, resources, and wisdom that can help us in times of need. Those who are successful in life (by no small measure due to your mentorship) are also typically extremely trustworthy and would want nothing more than to help their parents who've done so much for them. I'm happy my mom let me help her manage her cancer diagnosis. And I'm happy to report she has been in remission for two years.

Trusting your children with your financial situation is no different—it's scary, but they will likely surprise you with their thoughtful questions and desire to be helpful. As I mentioned earlier, if you have a child you know is a spendthrift or is struggling with addiction or mental health issues, clearly, that changes the conversation. In such a case, it may be best to explain to your child what you are and are not able to do to help them financially, but most importantly, it is best to stay focused on how to maintain an open line of communication with that child.

Author Rita Mae Brown coined the phrase, "The definition of insanity is doing the same thing over and over again and expecting a different result." For decades, parents have been unwilling to discuss health or finance with their children, so it's no wonder these are areas where most are still very unsure of themselves. With the overwhelming amount of information we now have access to online—most of which is ill-conceived and designed to sell you something—now is the time to try something different. My recommendation is openness and transparency.

Lack of communication adds another hardship when the parent needs end-of-life care or passes. Many times, adult children have no idea what their parents' wishes are. There is no list of all the banks, advisors, and brokers that Dad and Mom used. And some children don't even know the name of their parents' estate planning attorney. What kind of insurance policies do they have? Is the mortgage paid off? Do they have other obligations that need to be paid before the estate closes?

These candid conversations allow you to give your children the help we talked about in the last chapter. It provides an opportunity for the children who've been responsible to feel assured their behavior will be rewarded and to plan for how they can be helpful to the family at this moment of grief. Equally as important, the child who has taken his share of inheritance early will have an explanation for why the will seems unbalanced.

And while you don't want to overwhelm your young children with more health and financial information than they need to know, the earlier we start having age-appropriate discussions about both topics, the better.

Avoid Shock and Awe

The kryptonite for family dynamics is shock and surprise. Communication will allow you to leave the financial legacy you desire, and it will also preserve or strengthen the relationship between your children. One thing that will ruin their chances of that relationship is a surprise while they're sitting in the attorney's office after your funeral. When they find out their sister got the house or their favorite piece of jewelry goes to their sister-in-law, it can cause shock and resentment.

You thought you had everyone figured out. You never dreamed the entire family thought your niece should get that bracelet. And even though you left the house to the one child who rented because they weren't expecting it, your other two children who own their own home feel bitter because they thought they'd at least get a share. You never want your children to feel like they were penalized financially for being responsible and successful. That doesn't mean you have to leave an equal amount to each child or not provide disproportionate assets to a child who has special needs. It just means you need to talk to your children about your plans way ahead of time.

Shock and surprise, especially during this time of grief, is when things get ugly. You don't want your children to feel betrayed. Usually, the circumstances aren't sinister. It's just too little communication or miscommunication. The entire situation goes downhill even faster when the problem is the omission of communication. And in most cases, that's exactly what it is.

If you surveyed a room full of people and asked the definition of wealth, I think you'd get a variety of answers. Wealth looks different in every family. For many it goes deeper than the bottom line; it encompasses values and community.

Regardless of your definition, if you want to pass your idea of wealth along to the next generation and you want your children and grandchildren to remain friends after you're gone, initiating the conversation and setting up a communication plan that's right for your family is essential. Each generation must know your values as well as the various places you've stashed your financial wealth. Not having a communication plan cannot be an option. And the wealth creation generation has to become one hundred percent responsible for thinking about what the family dynamics will look like after they're gone.

This suspenseful type of will reading was common when my grandmother's generation passed. The news the children received in the lawyer's office might be good or bad, but not knowing was the norm. And almost every time, it caused family friction. Without this communication, no one is prepared and resentment builds. One sister did all the hard work of taking care of mom and getting the house sold when she went into a nursing home, but the brother ended up with the bulk of the estate.

You would never enter into any other significant endeavor without a blueprint. Yet this major life-changing event often gets recorded and never again discussed. Sometimes, family situations change, and the will remains locked in the filing cabinet. I'm still amazed at how many people think they don't need a will or an estate plan. I'm also surprised by how many people never change their plans even as their family situation changes. I work with extremely organized and well-advised clients, and still, they struggle with getting their estate plans right. This is not easy and can't be solved by one begrudging meeting with an attorney. As I've said throughout this book, focus, discipline, and motivation are the key elements of creating good savings habits, investment plans, and, yes, effective estate plans. Without a desire to see it done right, trust me, it won't be.

There's an unpopular quote that carries too much truth. "Shirtsleeves to shirtsleeves in three generations" speaks of the way one generation works hard to build a business and create significant wealth, the second generation thrives and builds on their parents' accomplishments, but the third generation squanders it away. I believe a major player in this unfortunate dynamic is the missing conversation. What if this phenomenon comes not from an irresponsible third generation but rather from the lack of adequately communicated best practices, family values, and lessons to guide the younger generation?

It doesn't matter if the legacy consists of millions of dollars or thousands. If the parents' intentions as well as their values and ideals aren't clearly communicated from generation to generation in such a way that those inheriting understand or are prepared to receive them, there's no chance of seeing them extend to future generations.

Many from the wealth creation generation worry that passing along a large estate will kill the ambition of future generations. Will your grandchildren lose the drive to put their talents to work if they have an abundance of financial wealth? The only answer to this dilemma is to impart your wisdom to your loved ones. They need to understand your work ethic and why you believe hard work and making the world a little better than where you found it are so important. This information won't transfer to them by example alone.

My father is an estate planning attorney, so I know a thing or two about the common traits present in effective estate plans. As you can imagine, my brothers and I know exactly what to expect. In contrast, my father told us that despite the fact her son specialized in estate planning, my grandmother was still uncomfortable talking about the subject, even with him.

Another family I know has had detailed discussions about what will happen when the time comes to sell the family home. It's the only asset their parents own. The son doesn't really need the money, but the daughter does. Regardless, they have a clear plan to sell the house and split the sale proceeds evenly after taxes. If the parents need elder care, the proceeds from the home will take care of them, and if there's anything left, the children can split the remainder. They've worked out every possible scenario so there won't be any surprises when the time comes.

Some might say, "It's just a house." And they would be right. But, no matter how complicated the asset mix, consistent conversation and scenario analysis are imperative for proper estate planning and family dynamics management. If the asset mix is more complex than "just a house," the level of conversation and the strategies required increase in frequency and intensity. In all cases, the sooner you start, the better off you and your inheritors will be.

In one Barna study, fifty-one percent of adults surveyed listed family as their top priority.[25] But do your conversations around finances reflect this priority? If they don't, start today.

CHAPTER TEN

Creating Good Habits

Curing these three diseases to create Financial Longevity comes through developing good habits. First, we build them in ourselves, and then we can leave them as a legacy to our children. For some, fifty dollars a month might seem like a lot. But could you manage making that deposit if you skipped one meal out with friends each month or canceled a streaming subscription? It's no different than giving up that donut with your coffee in the morning when you're trying to control your diabetes or saying no thank you to fried foods because your family has a history of heart disease.

The habits we create for health and wealth are more closely related than you might think. Duke University reported on a study in New Zealand that found a strong correlation between a low credit score and poor cardiovascular health. It's not that one causes the other. However, the personal qualities that allow people to live longer also give people a head start in understanding the need for discipline and sacrifice in saving.[26]

We Need More Education

Fortunately, many schools have begun to teach and demonstrate healthy eating. Some educators have begun to see how personalized diets can help children diagnosed with ADHD.[27] The right people are beginning to see the importance of educating children in the area of healthy eating.

I don't know about where you live, but here in Georgia, children don't receive any formal education in finances. They don't study it in elementary school or high school. Even a college economics class doesn't get into balancing a checkbook or lessons on how to handle credit. Of all the things public schools require students to learn, basic money management should top the list.

Do people think kids will learn these principles through osmosis or somehow absorb it? We teach our kids to have a rainbow plate before their fifth birthday. My older children understand that if it comes in a box, it's not nearly as healthy as something you pull out of the refrigerator. But they have this knowledge because my wife and I have instilled it in them since they were small. We can't expect our children to become financially literate if we don't give them the tools and resources they need to develop appropriate financial behavior. This lack of information causes dysfunction.

And it's not just children who need this education. Because it's never really been taught in schools, many spouses and adult children need lessons on appropriate financial behavior. Fortunately, this is an easy problem to correct.

I used to go to my kids' school on career day and use three jars as an illustration of spend, save, give. Each child would get a stack of Monopoly® money, and they had to come forward and decide how much to put in each of the three jars. After they struggled to decide for a moment, I encouraged them to start with the save jar and then put the amount they would donate to their favorite charity in the give jar. When they saw how much they had left to spend, many would go back and take some out of one of the jars.

I would love to see more lessons on personal finance given in the schools. There are many incredible exercises like the save, spend, give triad that give children a hands-on lesson in financial behavior.

One client set up a Vanguard Fund for his daughter when she got her first job. He told her if she put fifty dollars in it every month, he would match it. For a young adult with no other financial obligations, that was an easy challenge. But she learned the value of prioritizing that monthly deposit—automating it the same way we would our electric bill. By the time she graduated from college and was ready for her first major purchase, she had not only learned how to save but also had enough money for the down payment on her first car.

It's Up to You

Financial communication needs to begin early. We obviously don't want to burden our kids with our money problems. However, it's never too early to be transparent with children when it comes to money. Learning appropriate financial behavior should be a lesson as staple as tying shoes.

Having candid, age-appropriate conversations with your children will help them be better with their own finances when they get older. Plus, understanding what you can and cannot afford and the difference between the things we want and need can weed out some of those loan requests. One thing I'm really proud of is that we always made our kids purchase their own iPhones. Not only did it make them treat the phone more carefully because they had to save birthday money, allowances, and other nickels and dimes, but, even better, after they turned the cash over to reimburse me for the purchase, they had a satisfied but also slightly sad look on their faces. That look was exactly what I hoped for—they were proud that they could buy the newest phone but recognized the work it took to save the money, making parting with it hard. Those conflicting emotions stay with anyone who truly values the money they earn.

Instead of coming to us begging for money, our children should be asking how to build stronger character and learn the behaviors required to earn money themselves. Lao Tzu, the founder of Taoism, famously said, "If you give a man a fish, you feed him for a day; if you teach him how to fish, you feed him for a lifetime."

When I graduated from college, my parents reminded me of the many lessons they taught and demonstrated about behaving well financially. They didn't tell me to come back if I had a problem. In fact, their message sounded more like, "We've given you a supportive network. You have all the tools you need to succeed. Now, it's time to be an adult. Don't come back and tell us you couldn't do it." They taught me to fish. Now, it was my turn to feed myself.

Share the Legacy

When you visit the doctor, they ask about your family history. Did your grandparents have cancer or some other genetic disease? How far back does heart disease go in your family? It's important to pass this knowledge on to our kids as they start making their own medical decisions.

To create generational Financial Longevity, our children need to have that same information about their ancestors' wealth practices. If Great-grandfather built the wealth, the youngest generation needs to hear the stories of that wealth creation and be able to pass them along.

This educational aspect allows each generation to take ownership of the family legacy. They become a part of the bigger picture. Without this knowledge, they don't have the same commitment or sense of urgency to protect it. On the other hand, when they've heard the stories about the sweat and tears their great-great-grandparents put into leaving the legacy and understand the values and ethics that brought their family to this place in history, the younger generation begins to own it.

The Talmud, an ancient Jewish book of wisdom and philosophy, defines wealth as "not a matter of money, but a matter of mind: the truly rich are those who are satisfied with what they have."[28] Educating our children on those who came before them can help them develop this sense of satisfaction. It can help four and five generations of a family better appreciate everything their ancestors sacrificed to give them their present abundance. Learning about the adventure and journey that built the wealth has the ability to connect the generations and set the youngest up for an incredibly successful transfer of wealth.

CHAPTER ELEVEN

The Rewards of Healthy Financial Habits and Disciplined Wealth

I've said many times that the typical emphasis in the wealth management industry is on accumulation, not distribution. There is a constant refrain regarding saving, investing, and compounding, and much less talk about spending, donating, and gifting.

Adopting habits to increase our health span—living longer and healthier—only makes sense if you plan to enjoy those additional healthy years. Starting a second career, getting involved in a cause that you are passionate about, and biking through wine country are all things that would make the sacrifices for a longer health span worthwhile. But in order to enjoy it all, you have to have the Wealth Span to pay for it all. Would you like to seed the business you start with your grandchildren or contribute to the non-profit you're volunteering with? Maybe you'd like to fund a month-long biking trip in Tuscany. Because of the focus on saving and investing, when we finally reach our financial goals, sometimes it's hard to change our habits to allow ourselves to spend guilt-free.

There are many reasons to work hard to create a solid foundation for your health span and Wealth Span—security, longevity, peace of mind. Any of these make great motivators for putting your utmost effort into setting yourself up for your best life.

But I always find that in a list like this, one thing, maybe the most important one, is missing: Fun! After working, saving, investing, and planning, we deserve to enjoy life for as long as possible. In my opinion, those familiar sayings like "spend it while you can" or "tomorrow isn't guaranteed" miss the point. Those phrases imply we will run out of time. They encourage us to spend—recklessly, if necessarily—to enjoy the fruits of our labor.

Instead, I propose we spend guilt-free and responsibly for as long as we can. With a good advisory team around you, you might opt to take that bucket list trip in your fifties instead of waiting until you're seventy. With the right financial planning, the fun can start early and last well into your eighties or even your nineties.

Permission to Spend

We've talked a lot about developing discipline and good financial habits, making sacrifices, and committing to saving. But I've got great news. By learning these lessons and putting them into practice, there will come a time when you can give yourself permission to spend.

Have you ever seen a child stand at the side of the playground watching the others play because their parents told them not to get their clothes dirty? Fear of what might happen steals their fun. It breaks my heart when clients come to me with trepidation in their eyes regarding their financial future. Many have anxiety they've inherited from those external sources we talked about earlier.

I feel bad when people avoid vacations because of the "what ifs." *What if I take money out of my investments to go on a cruise? What if I don't have enough to live the lifestyle I enjoy now until I'm ninety? What if I need the money for hospital bills or elder care?"*

Obviously, we need to develop good saving habits and disciplined spending. However, if we've done a decent job of preparing for retirement, it's just as vital to create a plan that gives us permission to have fun with everything we've saved. The reason we sacrifice for so many years is so we can have freedom for as many decades as possible.

Finance industry professionals tend to keep the conversation focused on savings. They talk about investing and compounding, but few discuss this idea of spending. Spending, giving, and gifting are not top of mind for many of our peers. Without a spending component, the plans stay simple, but incomplete. What's the point of all the saving if we aren't going to spend at least some of it on ourselves?

No one comes to me and says, "Hey, Michael, I don't need any of this money I have invested with you. We're just going to keep letting it grow." That's an aspiration many people hold. They want their nest egg to go on forever. And while playing into a clients' fear of seeing their balance decrease would make my life easier, it would make my job much less fulfilling.

In my opinion, spending is your reward for doing the hard work for all those years. It's like allowing yourself to have a chocolate souffle at the end of dinner because you've exercised and eaten right for three months.

Most financial planners tell their clients they have to limit themselves to two to four percent of their savings each year. They use a clinical formula as if spending is a one-size-fits-all proposition. Physical longevity also frightens people into saving rather than enjoying their money.

But that's not the way we should view it. By looking through the lens of longevity, if you're thinking about buying a vacation home, having more years means we can spread the payments out over more months. Rather than thinking about how much your dreams will cost and saying, "I can't afford this luxury," your investments allow you to lend to yourself.

Coming up with fifty thousand dollars for that new car up front seems impossible. But if you've put enough into your investments, you can borrow that fifty thousand from yourself and pay it back over ten years. Now, you have your dream car without impairing your nest egg. Seeing people buying their dream homes, sending their grandchildren to college, or naming a garden at their alma mater are the most rewarding things about accompanying someone on the lifelong journey toward financial health.

Enjoying Your Legacy

In that vein of giving yourself permission to spend, I love it when retirees start to talk about how they can give to their children. Not in a co-dependent way as we talked about earlier, but in a way that allows them to watch their children enjoy their legacy.

Depending on how much you're able to put in your nest egg before you retire, you may know you'll be able to leave your children a significant amount after you're gone. But what if you could pay your grandchildren's private school tuition or take the entire family on a beach vacation? Yes, you could leave it, and your children could divide it according to your will after your death, but wouldn't you rather watch them enjoy some of it?

When you've overcome the diseases that kill Financial Longevity, you may have enough in your savings to help your children build their investments. Because the IRS allows your children (or anyone) to receive a significant amount tax free each year, you could save them money in estate tax by gifting part of their inheritance early.

This early legacy giving is often only possible if you've opened those lines of communication we discussed. Creating space for those bigger, more productive conversations gives you room to voice your expectations for your gifts and avoid disrupting the family dynamics.

There are a variety of ways to watch your responsible children have a better life because of your legacy. Each idea will depend on how much you've saved and what you want to do after retirement. There is no one right way to spend or leave your legacy. Be sure to seek out an advisor who encourages you to reward yourself for your hard work and dedication while also helping you seek out strategies that allow you to leave a legacy for your children and charity in the most efficient way possible.

Philanthropy

When you've taken time to create a healthy financial future for yourself and your family, you put yourself in a position to be generous. Each of us has charities dear to our hearts. Plus, this philanthropic element can help open the door to communication.

People often have a difficult time broaching the subject of finances with their families. Sometimes it's easier to start the conversation with our philanthropic endeavors.

All the principles of building wealth, starting a business, and vetting investments apply to the topic of philanthropy. But often, it feels less threatening both for the parents as well as the children.

For the parents, it means you aren't forced to divulge your balance sheet and share the details of the family fortune. And for the next generations, the power of being able to help others seems more natural than a lesson on wealth management. There's no wrong answer. If someone in the family brings an investment to the table for discussion, there's always a chance someone will make a bad decision. But the philanthropic side feels safer. You may begin with a charity with values or a mission that doesn't completely align with the family, or your first choice may not be as fiscally responsible as you would like. Even if you end up redirecting your charitable giving, the money you donated went to a good cause.

So, investing in the philanthropic side allows the parent to see which children allow their heart to lead, which ones are more cerebral, and those who aren't as naturally philanthropic.

In addition to being a great bridge to effective financial discussions, philanthropy can also be one of the rewards of disciplined saving and investing. For many of us, leaving the world a little better than we found it feels as rewarding as achieving the retirement goals we set when we started our careers. A secure financial foundation with health span and Wealth Span aligned provides the opportunity to volunteer, create a seed fund, or even endow programs and other initiatives to help others in need.

Again, how you approach philanthropy comes down to your "why." Why did you work so hard to save, sacrifice, and invest? If your goal was to enjoy trips, toys, and parties guilt-free, that's completely understandable. But, if some part of you feels an obligation to give back and show the less fortunate or those who do not have role models that anyone can succeed with motivation and dedication to creating good habits, then philanthropy might also be part of your "why."

Hourglass Syndrome[IP]

Some don't enjoy the rewards of their discipline as much because they fall prey to Hourglass Syndrome[IP]. Imagine the sands of an hourglass representing your life. Grain by grain, your life progresses, each representing a memory or a day. And while we might imagine life is over when the sand is gone, I like to think of the flip as the day we quit going to the office or move into retirement.

For those without a plan, this can be a very stressful time. Though they've saved well and prepared financially, they can't enjoy the rewards offered by this proverbial flip.

If you sold your business or turned the reins over to your children, that first day with no emails to answer and no texts to reply to can be more stressful than running the business. Even the folks who worked a blue-collar job and had their entire identity tied to their craft might find themselves facing Hourglass Syndrome.

It's awkward to start taking money out of those accounts you worked so hard to build. You filled the Hourglass nice and full, and though the sand is flowing slowly after you've flipped into your second phase of life, it still feels uncomfortable.

The vaccine for this ill feeling is planning. A sound cash management, investment, estate, and philanthropic plan creates a structure that helps ease the transition from saving to spending. Well-structured wealth continues to grow even after the sand has begun to fall. I can't stress this enough. Your investment allocation and the quality of your assets matter well into retirement. Many believe they don't need growth after retirement, but that is a mistake. We need a plan that is more balanced than while we were earning a paycheck yet still has a significant growth engine to provide inflation protection and a cushion for the unexpected. And as the plan begins to work the way it should, the anxiety brought on by the Hourglass Syndrome fades. We should be able to reap the rewards of our sacrifice and discipline without anxiety interrupting our adventure.

Financial Confidence Lets You Speak with Your Wallet

Tanja Hester, the author of *Wallet Activism*, explains that almost ninety percent of investors want their financial choices to align with their values. Only those who've put in the hard work of creating the strongest saving and investment habits have the luxury of even thinking about such an alignment. However, when you find yourself in a position to make your spending, investing, and gifting plans express your family values, it is a powerful and comforting feeling.

About fifteen years ago, several clients came to me with a request. All were entrepreneurs and family business owners, and all found their equity investment choices unfulfilling. "We don't want to invest in companies that don't align with our values," one said.

That was the con of owning extremely diversified equity investments like index and mutual funds. As the investor, you have no control over the holdings. These clients had a very clear understanding of what makes a great business. And they wanted their finances to support only those kinds of businesses.

That conversation was the catalyst for the creation of our institutional asset management business. We developed three concentrated, high-quality, focused equity strategies as the foundation of our offering, enabling our clients to participate in wallet activism before such a term existed.

Over the years, we not only engineered an investment philosophy with ownership of great businesses at its core, but we've also eliminated certain businesses from our universe of available investments because they don't fit our clients' values. We've also decided not to invest in companies that demonstrate poor labor practices, environmental irresponsibility, or poor governance from senior management.

Another way to express your values with your wallet is through philanthropy. As mentioned earlier, philanthropy is one of the true great privileges of financial independence. Thousands of worthy causes offer limitless opportunities to contribute or volunteer your time so you can pursue your passions. While most of the motivation behind living a longer, richer Wealth Span lies in creating a better life for yourself and your family, your philanthropic endeavors will allow you to leave the world a little better than how you found it.

Education is my passion. I teach an investment class at my sons' high school, and my family endows a teacher innovation fund at a local elementary school. As I've gotten more involved in education in my home state of Georgia, I realized there is no formal financial education required at any stage of schooling. To help remedy that, I've dedicated the proceeds of this book to help provide funding for financial education programs throughout our state.

Whatever your passion may be, I promise the satisfaction you may feel reaching a savings or investment goal pales in comparison to the feeling you get from giving back and creating something ten times more meaningful.

The definition of wallet activism also extends to include the scheduling flexibility that comes from financial security. In addition to choosing the companies you invest in, the type of company you'll work for or run, and the great causes you'll support, a strong Wealth Span gives you the privilege of deciding how you'll spend your time. As many have said (correctly, in my opinion), time is our most valuable asset. A strong financial foundation gives you the flexibility to control your time as you get older. Do you want to work three days a week? Would you like to retire and start a second career? Maybe you want to help one of your children start a business. All these options are possible when you bring your destiny into your own hands and are no longer limited by an uncertain financial future. Bucket list trips and dream experiences also become a reality when you control your time. For many, continuing to work—and earn income—is crucial to their Wealth Span, so the ability to structure your work to take time for special experiences is a potential best-of-both-worlds scenario.

In his research, Daniel Pink, the author of *The Power of Regret,* found that we often regret the things we don't do more than the things we do. He also found that regret is the most powerful human emotion. Pursuing a strong Wealth Span, supported by solid financial habits, gives you the confidence to chase your dreams and take chances. It gives you the flexibility to control your time, give back to others, and spend guilt-free. These are the rewards of being financially educated. Experiencing all this while also minimizing regrets will undoubtedly lead to a more fulfilling life.

PART THREE
Future

CHAPTER TWELVE

It's Time for Action

It is possible to have confidence in your future and know that your Financial Longevity is sound. We want you to experience exciting, wholesome, fulfilling, and memorable moments, and still feel like your finances are on solid ground.

Creating Financial Education Opportunities

Some worry that the next generation will become dependent on the wealth accumulated by the previous generations. What if our grandchildren get lazy because we've given them a comfortable life? We've seen just the opposite. The next generation has extreme ambition. They want to create and contribute. They simply need space to collaborate and take their ideas to the next level. Sometimes, they feel boxed in by the family business or don't have support to work outside those parameters.

Successful wealth transfer happens best when there's a commitment to education. The inheriting generation needs to be prepared to receive whatever wealth you intend to pass along. Sadly, many don't have the same passion to educate on wealth management as they do to make sure their children and grandchildren get a college degree. Financial education needs to be a pillar of the family mission statement.

We work with many people who have regular family meetings. They set an agenda and make sure a financial education element is included. Sometimes they invite speakers, but each one includes either asset management, estate planning, philanthropy, or some other specific piece that adds to the knowledge of the next generation.

I encourage everyone to become as financially literate as possible. One option you might consider is a program we developed to provide in-depth training in the basics of Financial Longevity. Our eight-module curriculum includes balancing checkbooks, understanding your paystub, budgeting, taxes, investing, retirement, and more. Currently this interactive course is available at Kennesaw State University here in Georgia. Every student can earn the credential thanks to an endowment we've set up there. The college version includes a module on understanding student debt. We talk about when to take it and how to pay it off.

The proceeds from this book as well as our community and advanced learning opportunities contributes to the non-profit that will ideally set up more of these financial education courses in middle schools, high schools, and colleges across the United States.

Financial Longevity's Ten-Point Investment Discipline[IP]

I presented these ten principles throughout the book; however, I include the entire list here to make it easy for you to review.

- Successful investing is a two-way street. Beyond having a firm grasp on how to identify quality investments, one must keep in mind that building up one's assets is, if not a lifetime project, onc that usually spans a period of many years. New cash should be added to investment accounts as faithfully and regularly as life insurance premiums are paid, irrespective of the outlook for stock prices.
- If new cash is regularly added to a sound investment plan, and if properly qualified stocks are purchased, the investor will normally have secured their commitments at fair average prices. What this portfolio may do price-wise over the next week, month, or even several years after their purchase is relatively unimportant. The trust test of soundness for the investment plan will be how much the market value and dividends have increased by the end of ten or twenty years.

- Keeping a long-term focus is one of the hardest things to do in today's investment environment. That is why, of all the qualifications for success in investing, none is more important than a firm mind. Investigating thoroughly and intelligently allows the investor to remain unswayed by every breeze, satisfied as to the soundness and progressiveness of their overall portfolio holdings. Remaining resolute and calm in periods of great uncertainty likely leads to the most favorable lifetime returns and keeps one from making emotional or premature decisions.
- Do not focus on a particular investment "style" or "trend," but rather on making solid and repeatable returns by owning the highest quality investments possible. That is a timeless strategy.
- For most long-term investors, there is only one objective: maximum total real returns after taxes.
- Achieving good investment results requires much study and work and is a lot harder than most people think.
- It is impossible to produce superior performance unless you do something different than the majority.
- Bear markets (aka bad markets) have historically been temporary. Share prices turn upward twelve months before the bottom of the business cycle.
- While innovation should characterize all enduring growth investments, the ability to make money out of innovation is of primary importance.
- Warren Buffett says that nothing creates and maintains wealth better than the ownership of a great business.

Recommended Resources

Books

The Psychology of Money by Morgan Housel

Financial Management for Beginners by David Stokes

The Millionaire Next Door by Tom Stanley

The Essays of Warren Buffett by Warren Buffett

Atomic Habits by James Clear

How to Invest by David Rubenstein

Where the Money Is: Value Investing in the Digital Age by Adam Seessel

Websites

Clever Girl Finances, Personal Finances for Women - CleverGirlFinance.com

Podcasts

Taking the Complex and Making it Simple - Michael Merlin

Endnotes

1 Greenspan, Jesse. *History.* "The Myth of Ponce de Leon and the Fountain of Youth." August 7, 2023. https://www.history.com/news/the-myth-of-ponce-de-leon-and-the-fountain-of-youth.

2 Basaraba, Sharon. *VeryWell Health.* "Life Expectancy From Prehistory to 1800 and Beyond." June 2, 2024. https://www.verywellhealth.com/longevity-throughout-history-2224054.

3 Vasan, Ashwin and Zhang, Wei. *CFPB.* "Americans pay $120 Billion in Credit Card Interest and Fees Each Year. January 19, 2022. https://www.consumerfinance.gov/about-us/blog/americans-pay-120-billion-in-credit-card-interest-and-fees-each-year/.

4 Lou, Allison. *CNBC Make it.* "The Rise of Fad Diets." January 11, 2021. https://www.cnbc.com/video/2021/01/11/how-dieting-became-a-71-billion-industry-from-atkins-and-paleo-to-noom.html

5 Scutti, Susan. CNN. "Living to 125 and beyond: Scientists dispute there's a limit to our lifespans." June 30, 2017. https://www.cnn.com/2017/06/30/health/aging-dispute-humans-live-to-125/.

6 Sullivan, Dan. *Strategic Coach.* "The Growth Mindset that Extends your Lifetime." February 26, 2022.

7 Armitage, Hanae. *Stanford Medical.* "Diagnosing Rare Diseases Using RNA: Q&A" June 3, 2019. https://scopeblog.stanford.edu/2019/06/03/diagnosing-rare-diseases-using-rna-a-qa/.

8 Daley, Lyle. *The Ascent.* "Credit vs. Debit: Here's what Americans Prefer." February 10, 2024. https://www.fool.com/the-ascent/credit-cards/articles/credit-vs-debit-heres-what-americans-prefer/.

9 Horymski, Chris. *Experian.* "What is the Average Number of Credit Cards." April 24, 2024. https://www.experian.com/blogs/ask-experian/average-number-of-credit-cards-a-person-has/

10 *Nurture Life.* "Healthy Alternatives to Common Foods for a Better Diet." June 14, 2020. https://www.nurturelife.com/blog/healthy-alternatives-common-foods-better-diet/

11 *Heart Matters.* "13 Small Changes that Add Up to a Healthy Diet." Accessed September 21, 2024. https://www.bhf.org.uk/informationsupport/heart-matters-magazine/nutrition/small-changes-add-up.

12 Clear, James. *Atomic Habits.* 2018. Avery:New York. Page 38.

13 Ibid. page 22.

14 Lynn at AMA Clinic. *AMA Clinic.* "How Often Should I Schedule an Appointment." April 6, 2022. https://www.amacliniclynn.com/post/how-often-should-i-schedule-an-appointment.

15 *Wikipedia.* "Dietary Supplement." Accessed September 21, 2024. https://en.wikipedia.org/wiki/Dietary_supplement.

16 Pisani, Bob. *LinkedIn.* "Stock Picking has a Terrible Track Record, and It's Getting Worse." September 18, 2020. https://www.linkedin.com/pulse/stock-picking-has-terrible-track-record-its-getting-worse-bob-pisani.

17 Klebnikov, Sergei and Gaza, Antoine. *Forbes.* "20-year-old Robinhood Customer Dies by Suicide After Seeing a $730,000 Negative Balance." June 17, 2020. https://www.forbes.com/sites/sergeiklebnikov/2020/06/17/20-year-old-robinhood-customer-dies-by-suicide-after-seeing-a-730000-negative-balance/.

18 Ashford, Kate. *Forbes.* "What is Bitcoin and How Does It Work? Updated May 21, 2024. https://www.forbes.com/advisor/investing/cryptocurrency/what-is-bitcoin/.

19 Polen Capital. *Roger Montgomery.* "The Quality quotient in Long-Term Alpha." December 2, 2021. https://rogermontgomery.com/the-quality-quotient-in-long-term-alpha/.

20 Robert Hum. *iShares.* "What is Quality Investing?" Apr 14, 2023. https://www.ishares.com/us/insights/what-is-quality-investing

21 Maverick, J.B. *Investopedia.* "S&P 500 Average Return and Historical Performance." Updated January 3, 2024. https://www.investopedia.com/ask/answers/042415/what-average-annual-return-sp-500.asp

22 Clear, James. *Atomic Habits.*2018. Avery:New York. Page 27.

23 McCarthy, Justin. *Gallup.* "Drugs have been a Problem in Family for 32% of Americans." November 21, 2021. https://news.gallup.com/poll/357134/drugs-problem-family-americans.aspx.

24 *CDC.* "About Mental Health." Reviewed April 16, 2024. https://www.cdc.gov/mentalhealth/learn/index.htm.

25 *Barna.* "Americans Reveal Their Top Priority in Life." March 14, 2006. https://www.barna.com/research/americans-reveal-their-top-priority-in-life/

26 Duke Staff. *Duke Today.* "Credit Score Can Also Describe Health Status." November 18, 2024. https://today.duke.edu/2014/11/heartcredit.

27 *ADDitude.* "Why Sugar is Kryptonite: ADHD Diet Truths." March 7, 2024. https://www.additudemag.com/adhd-diet-nutrition-sugar/

28 Schorsch, Ismar. *The Jewish Theological Seminary.* "The Morality of Wealth." November 25, 1996. https://www.jtsa.edu/torah/the-morality-of-wealth.

About the Author

Michael Merlin is the founder of Merlin Wealth Management (MWM) and a CFP®. In his twenty-plus years as an advisor to families, Michael has always focused on demystifying financial, estate, investment, and philanthropic planning for his clients. With extensive experience in multi-generational planning and advisory techniques, as well as asset management, Michael leads MWM and its clients to create customized wealth plans that are steeped in the values and best practices of each family.

In January 2020, Merlin Wealth Management joined Rockefeller Capital Management to marry their high standard for client service, proprietary asset management business, and multigenerational advisory practice with Rockefeller's legendary family-office services and resources.

Under Michael's leadership, Merlin Wealth Management has been recognized by Barron's, On Wall Street, Forbes, and The Financial Times. Michael has also been published several times in the Atlanta Business Chronicle.

Michael lives in Atlanta with his wife, Caren, and their two sons. The Merlin family places a priority on ensuring that their children understand the responsibility for giving back, volunteering together for projects with the Leukemia Lymphoma Society, the Zaban Paradies Center, and Creating Connected Communities.